STEEL DRUMS

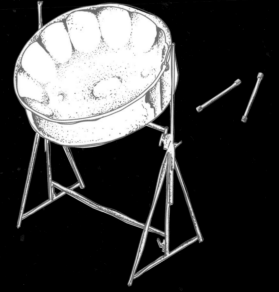

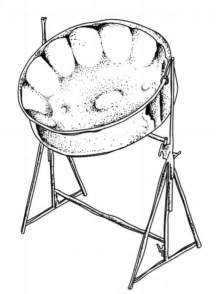

STEEL DRUMS

BY PATRICIA LAKIN

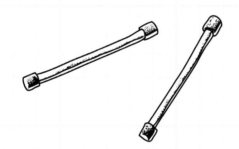

ALADDIN

New York   London   Toronto   Sydney   New Delhi

This book is dedicated to the pan players—especially the descendants of enslaved West Africans—who against all odds, restrictions, and economic boundaries found a way to make beautiful music.

 ALADDIN

An imprint of Simon & Schuster Children's Publishing Division

1230 Avenue of the Americas, New York, New York 10020

First Aladdin hardcover edition December 2018

Text copyright © 2018 by Simon & Schuster, Inc.

Front cover photograph of drum copyright © 2018 by David Field

Front and back cover drum illustrations copyright © 2018 by Elan Harris

All other cover photographs and illustrations copyright © 2018 by Thinkstock

Photographs of drums on pages 18, 19, 20, 21 and featured photographs on

pages 10, 11, 13, 14, 15, 17, 18, 20, 21, 22, 23, 24, 25, 27, 31 copyright © 2018 by Glenn Rowsey

Photograph of Carnival on page 28 and Panorama on page 30 copyright © 2018 by Alamy

Photograph of TASPO on page 30 copyright © 2018 by Getty Images

All other interior photographs and illustrations copyright © 2018 by Thinkstock

For information about special discounts for bulk purchases, please contact Simon & Schuster

Special Sales at 1-866-506-1949 or business@simonandschuster.com.

The Simon & Schuster Speakers Bureau can bring authors to your live event. For more

information or to book an event, contact the Simon & Schuster Speakers Bureau at

1-866-248-3049 or visit our website at www.simonspeakers.com.

Book designed by Lissi Erwin / SPLENDID CORP.

The text of this book was set in Univers LTD, Haneda, and AG Book Stencil.

Manufactured in China 0918 SCP

10 9 8 7 6 5 4 3 2 1

Library of Congress Cataloging-in-Publication Data

Names: Lakin, Patricia, 1944- author.

Title: Steel drums / by Patricia Lakin.

Description: New York : Aladdin, [2018] | Series: Made by hand ; 3

Identifiers: LCCN 2017007111 | ISBN 9781481478984 (hc) | ISBN 9781481478991 (eBook)

Subjects: LCSH: Steel drum—Juvenile literature.

Classification: LCC ML1038.S74 L35 2018 | DDC 786.8/4319—dc23

LC record available at https://lccn.loc.gov/2017007111

PICK UP A RUBBER-TIPPED STICK.

TAP THE SURFACE

OF A GLEAMING STEEL DRUM.

PING!

PANG!

pong!

EVEN AS A BEGINNER YOU CAN PLAY THE NOTES LIKE A PRO.

But playing an actual song to get that heart-lifting melody and toe-tapping beat—now that takes years of practice.

Can a person play a song on a drum? Yes! That's because a steel drum has a range of notes. And it's the only nonelectric instrument that was created in the twentieth century.

The steel drum is also called a pan. Ever wonder how it came to be or how it is made and tuned? In the following pages you'll discover how generations of determined and resourceful people from Trinidad refused to

let their music be silenced. Their passion gave birth to this percussion instrument.

You'll also get a behind-the-scenes look at how one man's musical path led him to make, tune, and play this percussion instrument. And you'll learn how he channels his passion to inspire youngsters to pick up that rubber-tipped stick and play pan!

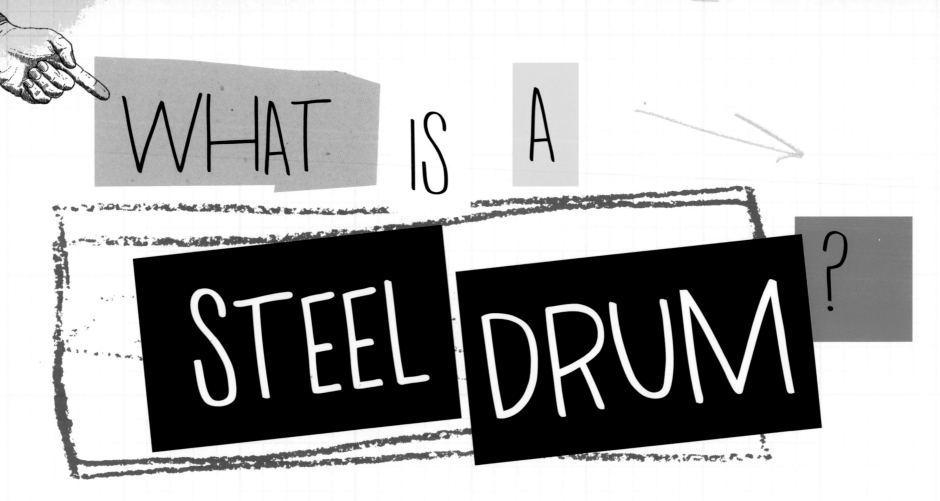

WHAT IS A STEEL DRUM?

FIFTY-FIVE-
GALLON STEEL
CONTAINER

EVERY STEEL DRUM BEGINS AS a fifty-five-gallon sealed metal container. The container is about twenty-three inches across and thirty-four inches high. These metal containers are made to hold liquids, such as oil. When an empty container is cut across the middle, it can make two steel drums.

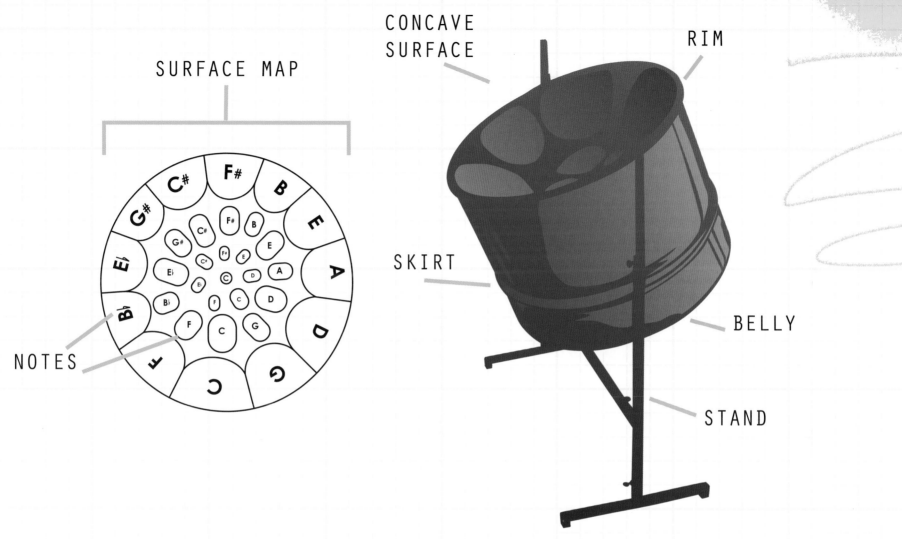

SURFACE MAP

CONCAVE SURFACE

RIM

SKIRT

BELLY

STAND

NOTES

The top of the drum is called the surface. The edge of the surface has a thin metal rim. The surface is concave, which means it curves inward, like the inside of a bowl. The notes are made by tapping a series of slightly raised rounded shapes on the drum's surface. Each shape makes a different note. The underside of the drum is called the belly. The skirt is the metal that encircles the drum. The length of the skirt determines the sound the notes will make. A shorter skirt gives a higher pitch. A longer skirt gives a lower pitch. The drum has two hooks so that it can hang on a pan stand. Pans have different names depending on the number of notes found on the surface. There are many different kinds of pans, including tenor, guitar, cello, and bass steel pans.

HISTORY OF THE STEEL DRUM

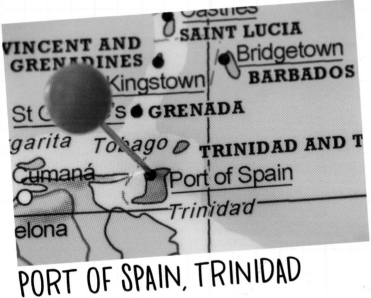

PORT OF SPAIN, TRINIDAD

STEEL DRUMS WERE BORN in and around Port of Spain, the largest city on the island of Trinidad.

This small Caribbean island is off the coast of Venezuela, which is in South America. Trinidad and steel drums are forever linked. That link may be traced back to the changes that followed after Christopher Columbus explored this area for Spain.

In 1498, when Columbus landed in Trinidad, he claimed this "new" land for Spain. But Trinidad wasn't new. For more than six thousand years it had been home to a large population of native people.

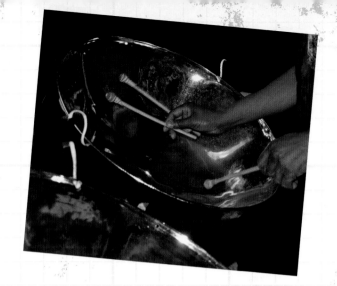

At first the Spanish, then French and later English settlers, created plantations in Trinidad. These settlers forced the native people to work on their plantations. By the late 1700s more workers were needed, so enslaved people, mostly from West Africa, were brought to Trinidad. Drums and drumming are tightly woven into West Africans' religion, history, and culture.

Once enslaved, the West Africans' one joy was playing on their drums. But drumming made the people in power nervous. Were those drumbeats a signal to revolt? Drumming was thought to be dangerous, so it was banned.

Britain took control of Trinidad in 1802. They freed the enslaved people thirty-two years later. The people were free, yes, but not free to play their drums. Over time Trinidad passed stricter laws banning drum playing. In 1931 they banned *all* African drums.

By then Trinidad's population included many descendants from West Africa. Instead of using drums, they made music by beating bamboo sticks on the ground or together. This style of music was called Tamboo Bamboo. Soon Tamboo Bamboo was also banned. But no one could stop their music!

Young people from Port of Spain's poor neighborhoods secretly gathered in backyards, which became known as panyards. These self-taught musicians tapped out beats on bamboo sticks, bottles, biscuit tins, paint cans, old car parts, and garbage can lids. But bottles broke and bamboo sticks split. Tapping on metal was better. The young musicians kept experimenting. What if the metal was heated? It made a richer sound! What if the tapping stick's tip was wrapped with rubber? The drum produced a warmer, less metallic tone. What if

the musician wanted to play a tune but the drum didn't have a specific note? They used a hammer to change part of the metal until the indentation created that note.

Bands formed from these panyards and competed with one another. Those competitions often led to bloody fights, cementing the idea that steel band players were gangs of troublemaking kids. It took a war to change that view.

Britain entered World War II in 1939, when Trinidad was still a British colony. One year later the United States was allowed to build military bases in Trinidad. Fifty-five-gallon metal containers, filled with oil to fuel ships and planes, were stored on those bases.

In 1946 nineteen-year-old Ellie Mannette was one of the first people to transform those empty oil containers into musical drums. He was also the first one to hammer the drum's surface inward, or make it concave, which had never been done before. This technique is exactly how all steel drums are fashioned today. Other musicians followed his lead. This wider drum's surface had room to etch out more notes than the smaller drums had. With more notes and more practice, these musicians went from playing a simple song such as "Mary Had a Little Lamb" to far more complicated tunes.

When Britain, the United States, and their allies declared victory in World War II, Trinidad made

Ellie Mannette, called the Father of the Modern Steel Drum, traveled to the United States because he was asked to train the US Navy's Steel Band. In the 1960s he was invited to New York by social worker Murray Narell to teach the steel drums to disadvantaged kids. In the process, Mannette's passion for pan infected Narell's two young sons, Andy and Jeff. These brothers are now famous pan players, composers, and teachers. Mannette's influence continues to spread. He is also the reason why West Virginia's Glenn Rowsey became a passionate pan man.

time for wild celebrations. Steel bands were allowed to join in. The joyous sound of the steel drums matched the mood of many Trinidadians. Pan players entertained people with popular songs and classical music. Steel bands were a hit! Soon after, in 1950, the Trinidad All-Steel Percussion Orchestra (TASPO) was formed. Ellie Mannette was one of the eleven pan players selected for this orchestra. Twelve years later Trinidad welcomed a now famous yearly tradition of steel band competitions called Panorama. The pans, and the people who made and played them, were finally appreciated and in demand in other parts of the world.

⌐ ANDY AND JEFF NARELL

11

MEET GLENN ROWSEY

BIM! BAM! BOOM! The sound of drums filled Glenn Rowsey's West Virginia childhood home. The drummers were his two older half brothers. At first Glenn just listened. By age ten he couldn't hold back. He picked up the sticks and began playing drums too. Glenn loved playing the loudest instrument, and beating out rhythms was joyous.

Thanks to his parents, Glenn was allowed to play drums at home for as long, and as loudly, as he liked. Being in the school band helped Glenn carve a solid place for himself. No one teased the kid who was such a good drummer.

But Glenn wanted to get even better. He began formal drum lessons when he was in eighth grade. He dreamed of playing classical music and enjoyed the music of Stravinsky. This twentieth-century Russian composer was famous for writing unique solo drum pieces.

In high school Glenn's drumming talent shone through. He made West Virginia's All-State Band, and he was accepted into the nationally renowned Drum Corps International. This program allowed Glenn to spend one summer with other teenagers crisscrossing the country giving drum concerts. The experience deepened his passion for drumming and gave Glenn the travel bug.

When it was time for college, Glenn's pick was easy—West Virginia University (WVU). They have a well-known percussion program, and the university is home to the World Music Center. It was in the music-school building that Glenn spotted a sign that would change his life.

GLENN ROWSEY & ELLIE MANNETTE

GLENN IN CAROLINA CROWN DRUM AND BUGLE CORPS

GLENN MAKING A STEEL DRUM

The sign listed a job offered by Ellie Mannette. The Father of the Modern Steel Drum had started the University Tuning Project at WVU and needed help building pans, or steel drums. Mannette was offering twenty-five dollars per pan. Glenn jumped at the chance.

Glenn was fast, did a great job, and loved the work. Mannette took notice. Glenn spent more and more time learning from Mannette. The first time Glenn played pans, he was jammed into a small classroom with almost forty other players. The raw energy and the amazing sound bouncing around that tightly packed room was unforgettable.

Glenn was hooked! He decided to stop taking classes at WVU and devote his time to pan-making by working for Mannette. He learned to build, tune, and play pans.

In 2007 Glenn opened his own business, called Rowsey—Pans and Pan Repair. It's located in Morgantown, West Virginia. But Glenn's business often takes him to far-off places to fix or tune a pan. That's because pans and pan players are now found in all parts of the United States and in all four corners of the world. What Glenn does, making and tuning pan drums, is an art that few can master.

When Glenn is on the road, he makes it a point to visit schools. It may be an elementary or middle school that has or is about to start a steel band orchestra. Or it could be a college where students are studying music. Glenn is there to answer their questions, give demonstrations, and pass on his passion for the pans.

GLENN PERFORMING

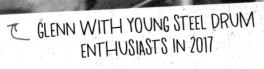 GLENN WITH YOUNG STEEL DRUM
ENTHUSIASTS IN 2017

THE TEAM AT MANNETTE STEEL DRUMS

HOW THE STEEL DRUM IS MADE

GLENN REMEMBERS THE FIRST time he made a drum, tuned it, and presented his work to his mentor, Ellie Mannette. "This is ready to go," said Mannette. Glenn knew that those five simple words were Mannette's highest compliment. His teacher's praise filled Glenn with an immense sense of joy and accomplishment that was hard to describe.

In Glenn's long, narrow, white-walled basement workshop, there are several fifty-five-gallon metal containers already cut and resting on wooden shelves. These containers never held oil; they were created especially for pan makers like Glenn. The one Glenn is working on sits on a small wooden table. His metal tool chest and air pressure hammer are close at hand. During two or more weeks of work, Glenn turns one big container into a shiny instrument, ready to be played.

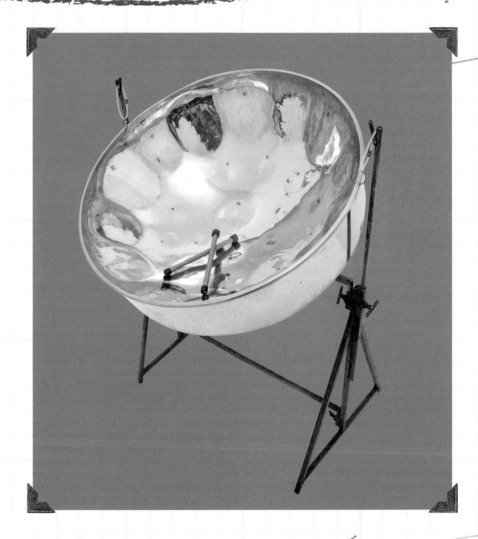

FIRST GLENN PUTS ON HEADPHONES TO PROTECT HIS EARS. THESE ARE THE REST OF THE STEPS THAT GLENN TAKES:

SINKING: Glenn hammers the surface of the barrel in a spiral, starting from the outer rim and working his way to the center. He's done when the center surface is seven inches below the rim.

SHAPING: With a pen Glenn draws the notes on the surface. For the notes closest to the rim, he uses a ruler and a compass. For the inner notes Glenn uses a template that was created by Ellie Mannette.

17

GROOVING: Using a metal punch, Glenn makes tiny groove lines around the inked-in notes. Each groove line is just one-eighth of an inch deep.

CUTTING: Glenn puts on goggles and gloves before he cuts the drum's skirt with an air-pressured metal cutter. Then he sands down the cut edge so that it's no longer sharp.

ELLIE MANNETTE'S TEMPLATE

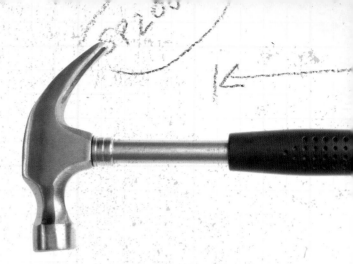

BUBBLE AND BURN: Glenn hammers the underside of the surface so that the notes he has made "bubble up" on the drum's surface. Then, with a torch, he heats up the surface. Heating gives the drum a richer sound. After that he lets the drum cool.

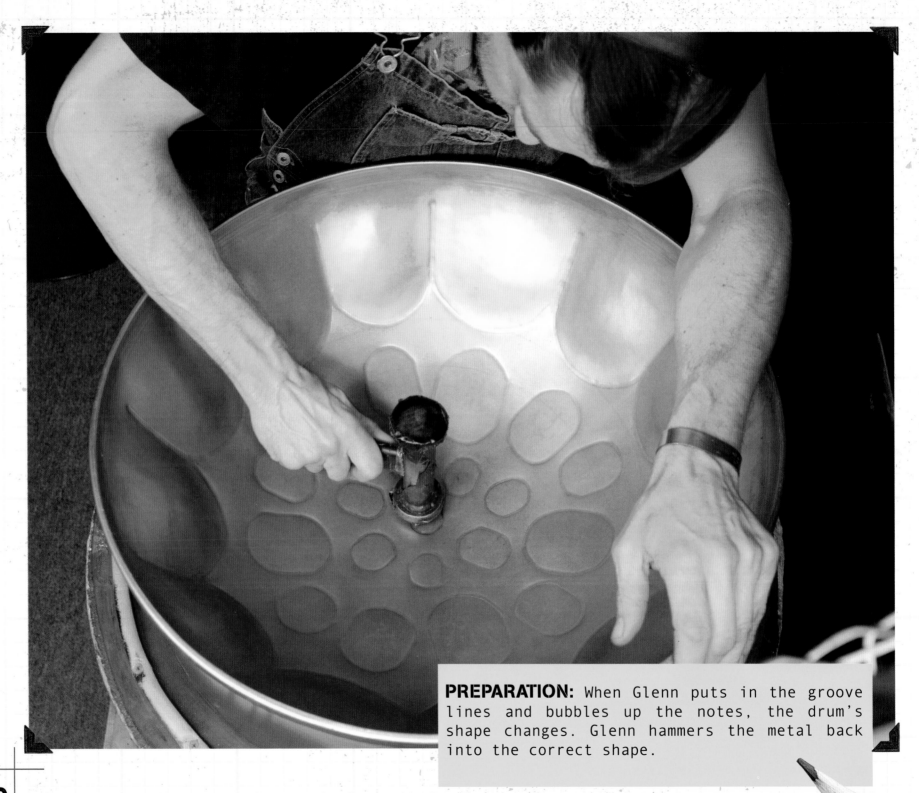

PREPARATION: When Glenn puts in the groove lines and bubbles up the notes, the drum's shape changes. Glenn hammers the metal back into the correct shape.

LINING: Glenn traces each note with a compass and labels it with a pen. Labeling lets the player know where each note is located. There is no standard method for placing notes on a steel drum's surface.

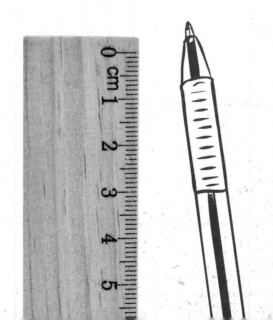

BUFFING: Glenn uses sandpaper to smooth out the metal grooves. Then he uses a buffer to get rid of any rust and to give the drum a shiny finish.

TUNING: It took Glenn years to learn and master how to tune a steel drum. Now he uses a padded hammer and some strobe tuner software to measure the pitch of each note. Tuning requires *tons* of patience.

Glenn repeats the "bubble up" step and gently hammers the notes from the drum's underside. The notes on the outer rim are done first.

Glenn hits a note. If the strobe tuner on his computer shows a line going up and down, then bingo! That note is in tune. But that doesn't happen so easily. Glenn needs to hammer away, then let the metal sit for a while, sometimes overnight, to let it adjust. Glenn keeps up this process for days and days and days. When the strobe tuner's line goes left, it means the note is flat. When it shifts right, the note is sharp. Days pass as Glenn gently hammers each note, until finally each note makes his tuner's line go up and down. Done!

CHROME: If the drum is being made for a professional musician, it now goes to a factory where it is chrome plated. That finish makes the drum shine brilliantly.

RETUNE: Once the drum has been chrome plated, Glenn needs to recheck each note to make sure they are all still in tune.

HANGING: Glenn uses a power drill to make two small holes—one on each side of the drum rim—so that the drum can hang on a pan stand.

GLENN MAKES ONE FINAL TUNING BEFORE SENDING HIS BEAUTIFULLY CRAFTED PAN OUT INTO THE WORLD.

NOW IT'S YOUR TURN

HEARING THE MAGICAL BEAT OF the drums as a kid was the spark that turned Glenn into a passionate musician and pan man. Today, as he creates this unique percussion instrument, he loves listening to top-notch musicians, whether it's jazz, rap, classical, or country.

What kind of music speaks to you? Do you play an instrument? Do you think you're not musical? Chances are that you did make music when you were very little. If you shook a rattle or banged on a pot, you were making music.

If you want to make music now, you have drums at home. They may be disguised as pots, pans, wastebaskets, and pails. Ask your parents which pot or pan you can use for drums. Take a wooden or metal spoon to tap out a beat.

You can also make simple instruments with other objects found at home. You'll be making music and recycling at the same time.

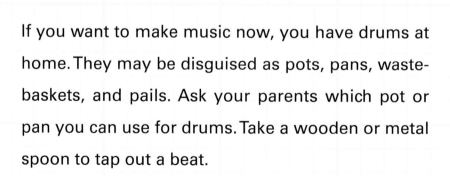

To make a drum of your own, use an empty cylindrical coffee or oatmeal container. Remove the lid. Cover the top with pieces of wide, clear tape. Make sure the tape is tight over the top. Take two pencils for your drumsticks and drum away. Experiment to make different sounds, just like the first pan players did.

For a guitar you will need an empty shoebox or any sturdy small cardboard box, elastic bands, and a ruler. Remove the box lid and place the elastic bands around the length of the box. Place the ruler inside the rubber bands on the closed or bottom part of the box. The ruler is like the neck of your guitar. Pick up the box and strum away.

To make maracas, a percussion instrument from Latin America, you will need two paper cups or two yogurt containers, seeds or dried beans, and wide tape. Put the seeds in one cup. Put the other cup on top of the first so that the lip of one cup touches the lip of the other. Tape them together. Lift and shake out a musical beat.

Are you like Glenn, determined to play pan? Where can you go for lessons? Ask a parent or teacher for help and do some research on the Internet. Who knows, someone at your school or at a youth organization you belong to might say, "Start a steel drum band? What a great idea!"

TIME LINE

1498—Columbus lands on the island that the native people called Iere. Columbus renames the island "Trinidad" and claims it for Spain.

1780s—Spain's rulers encourage French plantation owners from nearby islands to move to Trinidad. Many do so and take their slaves. The French introduce Trinidadians to their traditional pre-Lent celebration, Carnival.

1802—Britain takes the rulership of Trinidad over from Spain.

1834—People enslaved in Trinidad are granted their freedom.

TRINIDAD

CARNIVAL

1883—The British prohibit the use of African drums during public celebrations.

1889—Trinidad and nearby island Tobago are now both considered one colony and ruled by the British.

1900s—Music begins to be made by hitting bamboo sticks together or by beating large bamboo sticks on the ground. This music is called Tamboo Bamboo. "Tamboo" comes from the French word for "drum," which is "tambour."

1934—Tamboo Bamboo music is banned.

1939—The first steel band, Alexander's Ragtime Band, is formed and led by Carlton Forde.

1939—Britain enters World War II. All Carnival celebrations are banned in Trinidad because of the war.

IN THE EARLY 1900S, BAMBOO STICKS LIKE THESE WERE USED TO CREATE TAMBOO BAMBOO MUSIC.

WORLD WAR II FIGHTER PLANES

1945—The war ends, and steel bands perform in Trinidad's two-day victory celebration.

1951—Trinidad and Tobago's Steelband Association (created in 1950) forms the Trinidad All-Steel Percussion Orchestra (TASPO). This orchestra is made up of eleven of the best players from a variety of Trinidad's steel drums bands. That summer, TASPO travels to Britain to perform at the Festival of Britain and receives wide praise.

1957—While in Trinidad, US Admiral Gallery hears the steel bands performing. He becomes determined to create the US Naval Steel Band. Six years later Ellie Mannette travels to the United States to train the navy musicians.

1962—Trinidad and Tobago gain independence from Great Britain. Steel bands participate in the celebrations.

1963—To celebrate Carnival, Trinidad holds the very first organized steel drum competition, named Panorama.

TASPO IN BRITAIN

A PANORAMA STEEL BAND COMPETITION

1970s—Steel bands are formed in Trinidad and Tobago's schools.

1981—Biennial Schools' Steelband Music Festival is created to showcase the wealth of student talent in Trinidad and Tobago.

1990–1—Percussionist and professor Phil Faini of West Virginia University invites Ellie Mannette to be artist-in-residence at West Virginia University. The following year Faini creates the World Music Center at WVU.

1990–present day—Steel bands are sprouting up in many parts of the world. Pan players write and record their own music. They perform in such well-known places as the Apollo Theater and Carnegie Hall in New York, and in England's famed Royal Albert Hall.

THE LABORIE STEEL PAN PROJECT PLAYING IN ST. LUCIA

GLENN AND ELLIE MANNETTE, 2017

GLOSSARY & RESOURCES

BELLY—the underside of a steel drum

BUFFER—a mechanical polisher

COMPASS—a tool with a pen or pencil attached and used to draw a uniform circle of a specific size

COMPRESSOR—a machine that puts air or gas under pressure, which then operates a specific tool

> **AIR PRESSURE HAMMER**—uses a compressor to force air into a hammer's head to continually hammer the surface of a steel drum

> **AIR PRESSURE METAL CUTTER**—uses a compressor to force air into a metal cutter to continually cut the metal on a drum

MELODY—a series of notes that form a distinct tune

PAN—another name for the steel drum

PANYARD—a backyard where people play pan, or a rehearsal space where pan musicians gather to make music

PERCUSSION INSTRUMENT—an instrument that makes sounds by being hit, shaken, or scraped—such as drums, cymbals, and the piano

PITCH—in music "pitch" refers to how high or how low a note is

RIM—the round edging on a steel drum's surface

STROBE TUNER—a machine that measures the exact pitch of a note

SURFACE—the concave top of a steel drum, where the notes are

BOOKS:

Music from Behind the Bridge: Steelband Spirit and Politics in Trinidad and Tobago, by Shannon Dudley, Oxford University Press, 2008.

Steel Drums and Steel Bands: A History, by Angela Smith, The Scarecrow Press, Inc., 2012.

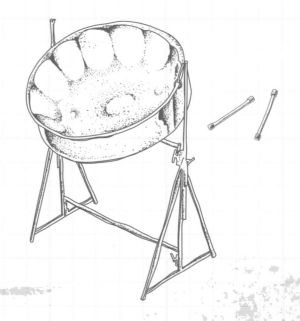